PRAISE FOR THE NAVIGATOR'S COMPASS

"A must-read for any leader, whether you officially lead an organization, a team, or want to have more influence in your own life. You can open this book to any page and find a wealth of helpful advice and food for thought. The Navigator's Compass is chock-full of practical, actionable advice. It is guaranteed to expand your thinking about your leadership. I found myself reflecting on many of the thoughts David raises in his excellent book, long after I finished reading it."

—Jesse Stoner
CEO, Seapoint Center
Best-selling author with Ken Blanchard of *Full Steam Ahead*

"David O'Brien once again sets himself apart from the rest with this tremendous work of clarity. The book is really a manual for leadership development based on practice, with foundations in theory. The real value of David's writing are the sets of premises followed by methodologies on how to achieve them. While leadership cannot be learned as simply as memorizing material for a course, his book provides a theoretical construct upon which to have leadership characteristics evolve, while effectuating the processes step-by-step via real-life, experience-based instructions. I would highly recommend his book to anyone who is, or may one day be, on a leadership path."

—Edward Rippel, MD
President, Quinnipiac Internal Medicine

"David O'Brien continues his directional theme for leaders in his second book, The Navigator's Compass. David's words transcend the traditional boundaries of personal and professional life to show that we are all leaders. This book is a quick, easy read with stories, lessons, and tips on a variety of leadership topics. You can read a chapter or the whole book and select the area or areas of leadership that resonate best to help you find your way. David provides suggestions for strategies to improve leadership capability and capacity to move us in our desired direction. With self-awareness as true north, The Navigator's Compass guides us to make informed choices and be the leaders and role models we continually strive to be."

—Deb Urbano
Vice President and Global Head
of Learning and Development
AWAC Services Company,
a member company of Allied World

"David O'Brien has mastered the essence of real leadership that is desperately needed in all corners of our society today. His writing style is smooth and easy. His extensive list of personal examples reinforces his message while his focused use of metaphors, analogies, and quotations adds brilliant color to every page. The Navigator's Compass is an extraordinary sequel to The Navigator's Handbook and moves Mr. O'Brien into the upper echelon of American leadership thinkers."

—George Hathaway
Best-selling author of *Leadership Secrets from the Executive Office*

"In the words of Andre Gide, 'We cannot discover new oceans unless we have the courage to lose sight of the shore.' The Navigator's Compass helps leaders to not only have the courage to take their leadership to a higher level, but also helps to chart the course and provides direction in the face of the prevailing winds of change. Author David O'Brien's great love of leadership learning and the lessons presented in the book help us to figure out how we can do great things within our organizations and within our lives. I highly recommend this book for any leader who wishes to increase their capacity to lead with influence and impact."

—Ron Cretaro
Executive Director
Connecticut Association of Nonprofits

THE
NAVIGATOR'S
◆——•———— COMPASS ————•——◆

THE
NAVIGATOR'S
◆— COMPASS —◆

101 STEPS TOWARD
LEADERSHIP EXCELLENCE

THIRD EDITION

DAVID A. O'BRIEN

PURPOSE
DRIVEN
PUBLISHING

**PURPOSE
DRIVEN
PUBLISHING**

Purpose Driven Publishing
141 Weston Street, #155
Hartford, CT, 06141

The opinions expressed by the Author are not necessarily those held by Purpose Driven Publishing.

Ordering Information: Quantity sales and special discounts are available on quantity purchases by corporations, associations, and others. For details, contact the publisher at the address above.

Cover Design by Nino Carlo Suico
Interior Design by Manolito Basta
Printed in the United States of America.

ISBN-10: 1-946384-07-0
ISBN-13: 978-1-946384-07-2
Library of Congress Control Number: 2017938665

The information contained within this book is strictly for informational purposes. The material may include information, products, or services by third parties. As such, the Author and Publisher do not assume responsibility or liability for any third party material or opinions. Readers are advised to do their own due diligence when it comes to making decisions.

Purpose Driven Publishing works with authors, and aspiring authors, who have a story to tell and a brand to build. Do you have a book idea you would like us to consider publishing? Please visit www.purposedrivenpublishing.com for more information.

To my dear mother,
who not only guided me to the Navigator's path
but also taught me why it matters.

To my dear mother,
who not only guided me to the Navigator's path
but also taught me why it matters.

CONTENTS

ACKNOWLEDGEMENTS

To Cathy O'Neill:
Thank you for opening the door and for providing me with so many opportunities to learn and grow

To John Honor:
Thank you for being a leadership role model for me and countless others

To Sherri Tanguay:
Thank you for asking really good questions and for reminding me that leadership excellence is a journey, not a destination

To my many other wonderful clients who have also become dear friends: Thank you for your support, encouragement and contribution to my leadership evolution

To all of my colleagues who continue to inspire me and teach me: Thank you!

To all who see leadership as a choice:
Never forget that you are the role model for the behaviors you wish to see in others

"If we would only give, just once, the same amount of time and reflection to what we want to get out of life as we do to the question of what to do with 2 weeks vacation, we would be startled by our false standards and the aimless procession of our busy days."

—Dorothy Canfield-Fisher
American author & essayist
1879–1958

Preface

The Navigator's Continuum

After my last corporate job as a senior vice president and general manager of an international consulting firm, a much-needed sabbatical was welcome. The time off for reflection was driven by a desire to assess what I had learned about leadership and organizational dynamics over the previous 15 years in Corporate America. The most important lesson discovered in this time of reflection was so simple it's hard to believe that it wasn't discovered until the sabbatical. While many factors had influenced my career success or failure, it all came down to behavior. It may seem obvious, but how one behaves in the wake of controversial management decisions, organizational change or shifting expectations determines career success or failure. We have a choice: Navigate through the maze of complex emotions and behave in ways that maximize our value; or react negatively and thus undermine our standing in the company and our potential for career growth and satisfaction.

When I first began my exploration of this workplace behavior—success correlation, I defined Navigating as *consistently doing the right things for the right reasons* or in the words of one of my most important mentors, "consistently taking the high road". While Navigating as a behavior choice continues to embody these definitions, I have expanded my thinking to encompass a broader definition. Specifically, I now see Navigating as *our capacity (and willingness) to consistently do more than is expected of us well, and with a good attitude.* This expanded definition is by my estimate, the critical building block of accountability and engagement. With very few exceptions, it is the cultural mindset of today's most successful organizations, regardless of industry or sector. Beyond the organizational value and impact of Navigating, I have also come to believe (and witness) that Navigating is a significant driver of personal leadership and job satisfaction. In choosing to Navigate, each of us is afforded the opportunity to not only create meaning and purpose, but also to use our influence in a productive way, regardless of role or job title. To be sure, Navigating allows us to be the role models for the behaviors we wish to see in others. In no small way, it provides countless opportunities to demonstrate leadership excellence in every area of our lives.

Since the release of *The Navigator's Handbook* seven years ago, I have embraced a learning continuum that has included countless conversations with leaders at every level as well as a significant amount of reading, writing and self-reflection. Although I have yet to define a single, magic formula for leadership excellence, I have been fortunate to uncover many new insights about what it takes to lead at a higher level. Even more importantly, this learning continuum has afforded me the opportunity to assess my own leadership capacity and its application in every role that I play. While I would like to be able to say that I've perfected my leadership, I cannot. I can however, with great clarity say that I have a deeper appreciation of the opportunities that the leadership path affords each of us every day.

Leadership is in fact a choice we make not just at work but in every aspect of our lives. In choosing to be leadership role models we uncover these opportunities in amazing places.

It is my sincere hope that this book will provide you with not only a few new insights, but also a few reminders of the opportunity you have to demonstrate true leadership in every role that you play.

Choose to Navigate,
David O'Brien
May 2017

About David A. O'Brien

David's Human Resources and Organizational Development consulting career spans 30 years and includes key leadership and P&L responsibility within a variety of industries including, Manufacturing, Healthcare and Financial Services. In his current role, David is responsible for providing Leadership and Team Effectiveness training, coaching and consulting services to organizations throughout the United States. His clients include such market leaders as Aetna, Advanced Behavioral Health, Allied World, Avery Dennison, Behavioral Health Network, ConnectiCare, CNC Software, Day Pitney, Dow Chemical, ESPN, Farmington Bank, Kaman Aerospace, KPMG, Mass Mutual, MetLife, Murtha Cullina, Otis Elevator, Peoples Bank, Robinson+Cole, St. Mary's Hospital, The Hartford, Travelers, United Technologies and Virginia Farm Bureau. He also works with many small and emerging market leaders as well as a wide range of non-profit and government clients to help bring about sustainable improvements in organizational effectiveness.

Prior to launching WorkChoice Solutions, LLC in 2000, David spent ten years with Lee Hecht Harrison, a global provider of business to business consulting services. In his role as Senior Vice President & General Manager, he was responsible for directing workforce management and executive development consulting initiatives at a number of Fortune 500 companies.

Before joining Lee Hecht Harrison, David spent five years with Oak Technologies, a regional provider of Human Resource consulting services. In his role as Managing Director, David was responsible for leading training and recruiting initiatives within the high technology manufacturing sector.

David's strong commitment to community service has resulted in him receiving several awards including Employer of the Year and Business Leader of the Year for his volunteer work. Currently, he serves on the Board of Mental Health Connecticut and is actively involved in several other community organizations. In addition to his undergraduate education in business administration, David has completed numerous professional development programs and certifications related to his profession. He is a frequent keynote speaker on the topic of leadership excellence and has lectured at a number of academic institutions including, UConn, University of Hartford, Quinnipiac University and the University of New Haven. His first book, *The Navigator's Handbook, 101 Leadership Lessons for Work & Life* is available on-line and in bookstores nationwide. Additionally, his articles have appeared in a wide range of local, regional and national publications and his case study, Leading Change from the Top Down is featured in the global MBA text book, Leadership Learning from Real World Cases.

To learn more about the scope of David's work in helping leaders and teams to be more effective or to arrange for David to speak at your next conference or other special event, please visit WorkChoice Solutions on line at: www.workchoicesolutions.com or call David directly @ 860.242.1070.

THE STATE OF LEADERSHIP TODAY

"I always wanted to be somebody but I should have been more specific." This famous Mark Twain line, while amusing, has more to do with the state of leadership today than one might think. Specificity as it relates to your leadership voice, style, and purpose is rapidly becoming both a necessity and an indicator of the times in which we live. It is in no small way a wake-up call for leaders at all levels. There is a growing tide of concern among today's workforce, which is driven by many factors including rapid change, the global economic crisis, absence of job security, and the overall state of world affairs. People are longing for something more, for meaning, and for a sense of belonging. This is at the core of today's leadership challenge and perhaps, more importantly, today's leadership opportunity. An opportunity that can only be fully recognized through expanded leadership thinking and clarity. Gone are the days in which leaders can rely solely on what has worked in the past. It is no longer enough to be externally focused. Today's state of leadership demands a higher level of awareness, clarity, and purpose—all of which require more frequent and deliberate introspection.

The awareness factor is by my estimation driven largely by the fact that true leadership begins from within. While writing my first book, I was struck by many important discoveries about leadership excellence, but chief among them was this truth. Without exception, every one of the highly successful leaders that I interviewed for the book shared this common denominator. First and foremost, they were life leaders. They were viewed as true leaders in all of their roles both inside and outside the organization. Does this just happen? Of course not. It takes lots of clarity and purpose, both of which result from self-awareness.

Being clear on who you are as a leader and what you stand for as a leader is a worthy goal to consider. It is important to note that your true leadership voice must include your true self. A common mistake that many of us have made (including me) on our leadership journey is believing that we must take on some other leader's persona. We think that we must subscribe to the latest leadership formula in the name of productivity, or worse yet, survivability in order to be effective. Nothing is further from the truth. The fact is that within every one of us is a true authentic leader. One that has the capacity to consistently do the right things for the right reasons.

Much has been written about authentic leadership, but one of my favorite books on the subject is *Authentic Leadership* by Bill George (Jossey-Bass Publishing). In it, Bill makes a strong case for the value and impact of authentic leadership, which, as he describes, resides in all of us. Finding your own authentic leadership voice takes more than awareness. It involves an ongoing commitment to exploration, experimentation, discovery, and learning.

The state of leadership today also requires leaders to explore the vast body of work on the topic of emotional intelligence, commonly referred to as EQ or EI. A good example of the urgency associated with this was illustrated at a recent conference I attended. A group of distinguished leaders was asked to identify the most important development in leadership thinking over their careers. Without skipping a beat, each member of the group said that emotional intelligence was by far the biggest and most important development in leadership thinking of the past twenty-five years. I wholeheartedly agree as it is a fundamental ingredient of authentic leadership.

There is a growing tide of concern among today's workforce which is driven by many factors including rapid change, the global economic crisis, absence of job security and the overall state of world affairs. People are longing for something more, for meaning and for a sense of belonging. This is at the core of today's leadership challenge and perhaps more importantly, today's leadership opportunity.

To be sure, there are a multitude of issues impacting the state of leadership today. While all of them have the potential to challenge the very best leaders, they also represent a terrific opportunity to build clarity and specificity. In knowing who you are and who you want to be as a leader, you may just discover your true leadership voice and purpose.

Five More Steps You Can Take Now

1. Consider these three questions: Who do I want to be as a leader? What do I want to be known for as a leader? What would it take to make this year my best leadership year ever?

2. Initiate a conversation with your peer group or a trusted mentor about the characteristics that embody leadership excellence and authenticity.

3. Identify one development opportunity related to your pursuit of leadership excellence and map out a series of small, doable steps that you will take between now and year-end.

4. Seek input from your team and other key stakeholders about what true leadership means to them and look for ways to apply the key behaviors of an effective role model.

5. Invest three minutes to complete the free Leadership Awareness Inventory on the WorkChoice Solutions web site at www.workchoicesolutions.com. Key words: *learning resources, leadership assessments.*

Redefining Leadership

Just as there are countless leaders engaged in the art and science of leadership today, there are no doubt countless definitions of the word *leadership*. Increasingly, I am asked to share my definition of leadership following one of my speaking engagements or workshops. As if I had fully solved the leadership puzzle, the persons asking wait in anticipation for what they must hope is a simple answer to their question. They might have been satisfied with the answer that I would have given a year or two ago, but more than likely, they are perplexed by my definition of leadership today.

As a beginning point, it is helpful to consider that there are distinct differences between management and leadership. Chief among them by my estimation is that management is more about the process or control utilized to achieve a specific outcome while leadership is more about the system that is utilized to achieve a specific outcome. Due to the complexity of human behavior and motivation and the critical reliance on human capital to achieve any business outcome, the broader system thinking context of leadership is often more relevant and effective.

For a very long time, I was of the belief that leadership was all about people and perhaps, more specifically, how one uses his or her influence to lead, inspire, and engage groups of people. While this still has a lot to do with my definition of leadership, it does not paint the full picture of what comes to mind when I attempt to define the word leadership today. In times past and perhaps for most of my career, I had defined leadership in a way that in hindsight was very one-dimensional. Namely, the single dimension of work or business. Not surprisingly, this single dimension was also limited by another singular view of leadership linked to one's job title. Like most people, I was of the belief that leadership capacity and opportunity were limited to people who had direct reports. After all, how could an individual contributor possibly be afforded the leadership opportunity let alone have the capacity to demonstrate leadership?

While this thinking still exists in many organizations today, the broader context of leadership has an even wider and more critical application for organizations both large and small. At an even deeper level, the world in which we live calls for true leadership outside of work too. Leadership today is by my estimation much more about the opportunity we each have to demonstrate personal leadership in all aspects of life versus the single dimension of work or job title.

With very few exceptions, most organizations today are grappling with the issue of employee engagement. At the very core of this universal leadership challenge is the unprecedented need for a higher level of personal accountability and ownership from all employees. A level of personal accountability best described as *consistently doing more than is expected well and with a good attitude.* Not surprisingly, this heightened level of personal accountability starts with the leader as he or she is the role model for the desired behaviors, attitudes, and performance. Being an effective role model in this context is not limited to leaders as every employee is provided with countless role model opportunities each day. To be sure, every high performing organization I've ever worked with or read about has managed to instill this truth into culture and action. In helping all employees to understand their full leadership capacity, organizations make huge strides in helping them to discover their own opportunity to demonstrate personal accountability and leadership. This is far and away the sum of leadership today. It is by my estimation the

> *"Allowing our values to guide us is an important part of developing our own personal leadership formula."*

level of engagement and leadership that all organizations s
but few fully achieve.

Discovering this opportunity of course does not happen by
chance. As a beginning point, it is tremendously important to consider one's core values and corresponding behaviors. While writing
my first book, I was struck by the clarity and resulting purpose that
this awareness created among highly successful leaders. Without
exception, these leaders were not just deeply aware of their core
values, but perhaps, more importantly, they were very clear on how
they lived these values both in and out of work. The result of which
was a deliberate form of leadership that allowed their values to
guide them each and every day.

Allowing our values to guide us is an important part of devel-
oping our own personal leadership formula regardless of our job
title, role, or level of responsibility. Beyond having values clarity, it
also helps to consider our intentions and the resulting purpose that
both create. When we choose to explore all of this, we are able to
access our full capacity to lead by defining our *true north*, which is
the sum of our values, intentions, and purpose.

As organizations strive for sustainable success in the years ahead,
it might make sense to consider the broader context of leadership. In
doing so, they may just help their employees to discover their own
opportunity to demonstrate personal accountability and leadership.

Ten Strategies For Accessing Your Full Leadership Capacity:

1. Find your *true north* (by considering your values, intentions, and purpose.
2. Define who you want to be as a leader and what others expect of you as a leader.
3. Examine and challenge your negative self-talk.
4. Look for more "role model" opportunities each day.
5. Make an effort to shut off the "auto pilot"—work hard at being fully present.

6. Count your blessing more often—develop a deeper sense of gratitude.

7. Keep a journal of your leadership journey.

8. Give yourself permission to develop your own leadership formula for work and life.

9. Calibrate your compass every morning through ten minutes of deliberate self-reflection.

10. Develop a sense of accomplishment and success by taking small steps toward your leadership development goals regardless of your job title.

Leadership Influence and the Role Model Opportunity

"Example is not the main thing in influencing others, it's the only thing." This almost famous but certainly memorable quote from Pulitzer Prize winner Albert Schweitzer offers an inspiring view into an often overlooked realm of leadership. Namely, the critical role that leadership influence plays in both getting employees engaged and keeping them engaged.

Several years ago, I began exploring the realm of leadership influence at the suggestion of a good friend who also happened to be one of my clients. For as long as I can remember, I have had what some might call an innate curiosity about human influence. Not just in the context of leadership or work, but in the broader context of life and behavior in general.

One of my earliest recollections of observing influence and perhaps, more powerfully, experiencing influence occurred when I attended my very first live concert. Despite the fact that the ensuing years have blurred such details as the name of the band, the songs played, or even the actual venue, the influence and resulting power of the bandleader remains crystal clear. Without exception, every member of the band, all ten or so musicians, were in hindsight, fully transfixed by the bandleader before and after each song. The source of this by my estimation even then was the influence that the bandleader seemed to have on each musician. I recall I was amazed that this happened with minimal verbal communication. It appeared to be a deeper level of communication that was somehow connected to the bandleader's attitude and behavior. Beyond being a highly skilled musician, the bandleader displayed tremendous confidence not just in where he was taking the group with each song, but also in their ability to get there with ease and musical finesse.

Fast forward thirty years. When my good friend and client suggested that I explore the realm of leadership influence, I had no idea where this journey would take me. At first glance, I discovered that leadership influence could be classified in two ways. One was what I came to call *productive influence* and the other, not surprisingly, I labeled *destructive influence*. To be sure, every person that reads this article will quickly be able to build a corresponding list of characteristics or at least adjectives that fit with either categorization.

In short, productive influence is about a higher standard of leadership that is among other things based on respect, trust, and integrity. The destructive influence by contrast is based largely on ego, fear, control, and, more than likely, self-doubt at some level.

For those not familiar with my work and leadership musings, it is important to note that I am a big fan of leadership quotes. This is mainly because the meaningful quotes force us to think. One of my favorites that underscores the power of influence is by well-known leadership thinker and renowned HR executive John C. Honor, who once said, "Everything a leader does or doesn't do impacts employee engagement and morale at some level." Although I heard this for the first time eight years ago, it is one of those quotes that continue to make me and other leaders think.

If everything a leader does or doesn't do is in some way a role model behavior, does it stand to reason then that everything *anyone* does is a role model behavior? This is a question that I have pondered for a good part of the past year, and one that I have asked many leaders during this time. It is also a question

> *In short, productive influence is about a higher standard of leadership that is among other things based on respect, trust, and integrity.*

that has helped to expand my view of influence while also adding new meaning to the term *role model*.

As a beginning point, every one of us, regardless of job title, is observed by countless people each day both in and out of work. As a result, every one of us is modeling roles with particular behaviors at every juncture. The overriding question however is, "What behavior are we applying as a role model? Is it behavior that inspires others, builds trust, honors differences, or motivates people to be at their best? This overriding question is by my estimation one that we need to ask ourselves not just daily but perhaps hourly. If we as leaders are to inspire our teams and others to achieve great things, we must be ever mindful of the power of our influence through our behaviors. A stunning example of this and the range of role model behaviors we observe each day played out in front of me just recently.

Early last month, I had the good fortune of delivering a full-day version of my emotional intelligence workshop to a group of twenty-seven early career, high potential leaders at a local employer. Shortly before the morning break, the topic of leadership influence surfaced. Ironically, I was only a few minutes away from raising the topic as part of the workshop content.

The question posed by one of the high-caliber young professionals had to do with whether or not a leader's influence goes beyond the boundaries of work.

Just that morning on my way to the workshop, I had stopped at a local convenience store to pick up a cup of coffee for my thirty-minute commute. I told the group that while I was in line waiting to pay for my coffee, I observed that the person in front of me was being very condescending to the cashier. As I waited for my turn and continued to observe this rude behavior toward the clerk, the thought occurred to me that this person was *in fact being a role model for others* in the store. Certainly not a positive role model, but nonetheless, a role model.

This realization convinced me that not only was I a role model here too, but in truth, this role model opportunity had absolutely nothing to do with my job title or the number of employees that report to me. After sharing this story, I asked the group for their thoughts on the original question. To my pleasant surprise, all but a few of the participants agreed that not only does a leader's influence go beyond the boundaries of work, but perhaps even more importantly, everyone is a role model. The difference between being a productive role model or a destructive role model is all about *how we choose to use our influence.*

Five Steps You Can Take Now To Affect Your Influence

1. Consider how you use your influence and what impact it has on team engagement and overall morale.
2. Initiate a conversation with your peer group about the power and reach of leadership influence and work to identify examples of productive and destructive influence.
3. Seek input from your team and other key stakeholders about the range of role model opportunities that are presented to them on a daily basis. Also identify the key behaviors that support being a positive role model in each example.
4. Invest three minutes to complete the free Leadership Influence Survey on the WorkChoice Solutions web site at www.workchoicesolutions. Key words: *learning resources, leadership assessments.*
5. Identify one personal development opportunity related to your leadership influence and map out a series of small, doable steps that you will take between now and year-end to expand your leadership influence.

THE CALL TO LEADERSHIP
IN TURBULENT TIMES

Today's often frantic pace of business, aptly described by many as "permanent whitewater," has never before produced such a need for true leadership. Add to this the fallout from the current global economic crisis, and this need has shifted to an all-out clarion call for leaders to rise to a higher level of leadership thinking and action.

Remarkably, this whitewater pace has also produced an unparalleled opportunity for leaders and teams to become more fully engaged and to collectively reap the benefits of good leadership practices. Herein lies perhaps the first shift in leadership thinking that can guide today's leader onto the path to great leadership. To be sure, the multitude of distractions that most leaders face today can, and often do, inhibit the capacity to see, let alone discover, this opportunity. With the alternative encompassing such outcomes as lost productivity, burnout, and even business failure, it makes good sense for leaders to explore the upside of today's whitewater pace.

Expanding one's thinking to include a broader view of what leadership really means to both the leader and his/her team is another important embarkation point on the journey to great leadership. Napoleon once said that "true leaders are dispensers of hope." Clearly, if there was ever a time when your team needed hope, it's now. In fact, it's probably safe to say that your team is hungry for hope. After all, the good news deficit in many organizations today is at an all-time high. Take the good news deficit test in your world of work. Simply assess the ratio of good news to bad news (rumor mill included) that your employees see, hear, or read in a given week. More than likely, the good news deficit in your organization is fairly high too. Good leadership is of course more than this, but it's an important consideration as you help your team to discover the opportunity.

Exploring the values connection among your team is a meaningful starting point in the shift from a new level of leadership thinking to a new level of leadership action. In all of my twenty plus years as a student of leadership, I have yet to discover a more powerful way of building community and increasing engagement. Simply put, when employees are grounded and guided by shared values, they produce better outcomes and are able to navigate the turbulent waters of change and ambiguity with ease and grace. Taking the time to examine your leadership thinking and related actions is not just good leadership, it's good business too. As we make our way through the whitewaters of leadership in the twenty-first century, we may just learn to sail if we honor the huge responsibility of the leadership path. Our teams and our careers are counting on it.

Five More Steps You Can Take Now

1. Initiate a discussion with your team about their view of leadership and what they think are the key characteristics of great leadership. Look for linkage to your leadership strategy.
2. Seek feedback from your team and peer group about the good news deficit at your organization and encourage everyone to share ideas on how to reduce or eliminate the deficit across your team and organization.
3. Seek feedback from a trusted friend/colleague about your leadership blind spots.

Expanding one's thinking to include a broader view of what leadership really means to both the leader and his/her team is another important embarkation point on the journey to great leadership.

4. Incorporate a "values discussion" in your next staff meeting and encourage your team to identify the top three shared values of the group.

5. Make a list of all of the things that your team does well and acknowledge each person's contribution to your success.

LEADERSHIP ENGAGEMENT AS JOB ONE

The demands of today's *more with less* workplace climate have produced an unprecedented amount of stress and frustration in most people's lives. Not surprisingly, these dynamics are magnified substantially in the lives of countless leaders who are expected to foster a culture of *work harder, smarter*, and *faster*. At the very core of this not so new but accelerating workplace reality is the issue of employee engagement. While much has been written and continues to be written about this subject, the often overlooked reality is that employee engagement starts with leadership engagement.

Countless engagement surveys are conducted every year, and in most cases, the focus is on employee gaps in productivity and overall performance. Of course there is value in most of these surveys but without a deeper understanding of the leader's role, the potential for peak performance among the broader team is marginal at best.

As a beginning point, leaders must assess their own level of engagement based on such critical leadership characteristics as openness, integrity, resilience, trust, respect, and overall role model behavior. Absent a high level of commitment to these important factors, leaders at any level will be fighting an uphill battle to inspire and motivate a higher level of employee engagement.

Taking the time to understand the complexities of employee motivation is another worthwhile endeavor for today's leader. While writing my first book, I conducted a fairly rigorous research effort that explored how employee motivation had evolved over the previous twenty-five years. There were certainly some interesting findings in my research, but chief among them was the influence that *feeling valued* had on employee motivation and engagement. To be sure, there are a multitude of factors that influence employee motivation, but today's leader is well served by choosing to explore this and its critical link to high performance.

Creating clarity through clear and consistent communication especially as it relates to performance expectations also goes a long way in building employee engagement. While there are certainly core characteristics that describe what employee engagement means in general terms, there are in fact elements that are unique to each organization and/or team. Soliciting input from employees regarding team specific measures helps to not only build a common language, but also creates purpose and more than likely ownership too.

Another important element of the clear and consistent communication equation is the leader's ability to link each person's role and contribution to the key goals of the department and organization. The more each employee understands how their efforts impact the greater good of the group, the more likely they are to find meaning in their work.

The issue of clarity goes well beyond building a framework of understanding as it relates to performance expectations. Timely and specific feedback also serves to guide each employee toward a higher level of engagement and personal success. Acknowledging the fact that no employee knowingly chooses to fail can, and often does, set the tone for marked improvements in engagement and job ownership.

Employee engagement is clearly the engine that drives high performance. While conventional thinking tends to focus on the employee as the starting point, leaders within all functions must understand and embrace their role in this equation based in large part on the enormous range and scope of their influence. Absent a high level of leadership engagement, it's mere folly to expect high performance from individuals or teams.

Six More Steps You Can Take Now

1. Define the top five leadership characteristics that best describe your leadership formula and assess the impact that they have on employee engagement.

2. Initiate a discussion with your team about their view of engagement and what they think are the key actions and behaviors that support success for the group and organization.

3. Seek input and guidance from your human resource partners to assess your leadership gaps and to develop meaningful solutions for increasing employee engagement in your department.

4. Assess the frequency and impact of your leadership communications to identify areas of improvement. Think, *what can I do more of* and *what should I do less of.*

5. Incorporate an "employee motivation discussion" in your next staff meeting and encourage your team to identify the top three shared motivation drivers of the group.

6. Invest the time to identify linkage between each person's role and the key objectives of your department. Communicate this clearly and often.

At a beginning point, leaders must assess their own level of engagement based on such critical leadership characteristics as openness, integrity, resilience, trust, respect and overall role model behavior. Absent a high level of commitment to these important factors, leaders at any level will be fighting an uphill battle to inspire and motivate a higher level of employee engagement.

THE THREE CRITICAL
DIMENSIONS OF EI

"The new gold standard of leadership success is one's capacity to build and maintain meaningful relationships through human connection." This powerful insight from leadership crusader Lyle Winslow offers a stunning glimpse into a multitude of universal leadership truths today. As a beginning point, it reminds us that the measure of our success as leaders continues to evolve. At another level, it calls us to reexamine our leadership thinking and success formula. Even more importantly, and at a much deeper level, it offers us a guidepost to a higher level of leadership in all of our roles.

Creating human connection by most estimates is not only a worthwhile endeavor, but also a critical leadership competency deeply rooted in emotional intelligence. While many of the foundational aspects of true leadership remain constant, today's do-more-with-less business climate demands a higher level of emotional intelligence than ever before.

Much has been written about emotional intelligence since the mid-1990s when pioneers like Daniel Goleman, Robert Cooper, and Peter Salovey first introduced the EI concept. At its simplest level, EI is the combined sum of an individual's social and interpersonal skills. It also encompasses one's ability to sense, understand, and influence other people.

In the broadest context, EI competence includes such factors as self-awareness, self-regulation, interpersonal skills, motivation, influence, empathy, and acceptance of diversity. While all of these have a tremendous impact on a leader's ability to create human connection, the self-awareness factor offers the most direct pathway to recognizing the full benefit of emotional intelligence. Even more significant is that absent the self-awareness factor, leaders are unlikely to discover the human connection correlation to leadership excellence.

One of the most prevalent leadership truths today is that, with very few exceptions, employees long for meaning in their work. They want to be part of something bigger than themselves, and they want to believe in the future. This by my estimation is at the core of the human connection opportunity presented to all leaders.

Being self-aware while critically important to leadership success is but the first step in being able to create meaningful human connection. One of the most common barriers to creating human connection is a lack of self-regulation among the leadership ranks. Despite the fact that workplace stress is at a near epidemic level in most organizations today, leaders need to be the positive role models for navigating stress and change at every juncture. Additionally, they need to be well aware of their various emotional states and the corresponding triggers that move them beyond emotional self-control or regulation. When we as leaders neglect to manage our negative emotions, most of which are normal, we also neglect the opportunity to create meaning and purpose for our teams.

Although empathy, like the word leadership, means different things to different people, one thing that is certain is that empathy arises from respect. Absent respect, it is difficult to develop a sensitivity of other's feelings, needs, and concerns, all of which open the way to human connection. When employees feel respected and when their human condition is validated, they are far more likely to be engaged and hopeful.

Not surprisingly, empathy like self-awareness and self-regulation requires deliberate effort on the part of the leader.

> *"The new gold standard of leadership success is one's capacity to build and maintain meaningful relationships through human connection."*
> —*Lyle Winslow*

It also requires openness to diverse perspectives and an appreciation of the fact that we all long for meaningful human connection and the sense of belonging that it creates.

As we make our way through the whitewater pace of business today, let us remain hopeful and committed to building our emotional intelligence. In doing so, we may just discover our true capacity to create meaningful human connection in all areas of our lives.

Ten More Steps You Can Take Now

1. Invest the time to consider your core values and what you stand for as a leader.
2. Identify your different emotional states and define key drivers of each.
3. Consider how you use your influence and what impact it has on others.
4. Avoid making snap remarks and decisions—use the count to ten rule.
5. Slow down a bit and don't interrupt—utilize an association technique to stay grounded.
6. Learn and apply healthy stress busting techniques.
7. Assume positive intent.
8. Seek first to understand—keep biases in check.
9. Resist the urge to focus solely on differences.
10. Invest five minutes to complete the free EI Insights Inventory on the WorkChoice Solutions web site at www.workchoicesolutions.com. Key words: *learning resources, leadership assessments.*

Think, Exploring the Value
of Think Time

When was the last time you really took the time to think? If you're like most busy leaders I know, you probably said just a few minutes ago or possibly only a few hours ago. You might even be quick to respond that you're thinking right now as you read these words. If I had been asked this question only a year or two ago, I would have likely responded the same way. I might have even been annoyed by such an inquiry. After all, as leaders, we get paid to think. While there is a great deal of truth to this, the deeper truth is that few of us rarely take the time to think about an issue for more than a few seconds or minutes. There are of course exceptions, but more times than not, today's multitasking leader races through the thinking process in the name of efficiency.

To be sure, success in any worthwhile endeavor demands good thinking. To move forward as leaders, we must be willing and able to analyze information accurately, anticipate the consequences of options, and to draw reasonable conclusions. We also need to be able to explain our points of view by providing good reasons and, at times, solid evidence. Not surprisingly, all of this takes more than a few seconds or minutes to ensure a successful outcome. By my estimation, it takes even more than what is commonly referred to as *critical thinking*.

Critical thinking is the capacity to make timely, effective, and well-reasoned decisions, which are all absolutely essential for leadership success. Much has been written about critical thinking, but a good frame of reference comes from author David T. Moore, who defines *critical thinking* as "a deliberate metacognitive (thinking about thinking) and cognitive (thinking) act whereby a person reflects on the quality of the reasoning process simultaneously while reasoning to a conclusion." He goes on to say that the thinker has two equally important goals: coming to a solution and improving the way she or he reasons. Hence, critical thinking means much more than logic.

Several years ago, I was involved in the delivery of an eight-module leadership series for a Hartford-based client. To demonstrate the organization's commitment to the initiative, a member of the executive team did the kickoff of each workshop. For the final workshop in the two-year series, the chairman of the company did the kickoff segment. He was by all accounts a highly respected global leader with an impressive record of success over his forty-year career. Even more importantly, he was widely known as an authentic leader who allowed his core values to guide him at every juncture.

Before the final workshop began, the two of us had nearly thirty minutes to review our presentations in an effort to create linkage between the two presentations. Knowing that I was in the presence of a true leader, I decided to seek his guidance about leadership. I was certain that even a single nugget of leadership wisdom from him would be quite meaningful. In hindsight, it was one of the most meaningful nuggets of leadership wisdom I've heard in a very long time. When asked "what is one piece of advice you would give to a leader as he or she begins their leadership journey," he replied, "Take the time to think." I must admit that, at first, I was a bit perplexed. I guess that I had expected something related to core values, emotional intelligence, or even faith, but certainly not the idea of "thinking."

> *Our intellect requires a voice, and thinking gives it that voice. In making deliberate think time a part of your daily routine, you not only create greater clarity, purpose, and meaning for yourself, but also for your team.*

After what seemed to be a very long pause, he went on to say that few of us rarely take the time to think. The absence of deep and deliberate thinking by his estimation had become a hurdle for both leaders and organizations.

While this leadership insight made some sense the first time I heard it, the truth is that it has become a very important part of my development both as a leader and a consultant. Taking the time to think, to really think about important issues, has made the difference between seeing a limited range of options and seeing multiple options. Not surprisingly, it has also produced greater clarity and better outcomes.

Each of us is provided with numerous opportunities every day to harness our intellectual capacity by thinking in a deliberate way. Our intellect requires a voice, and thinking gives it that voice. In making deliberate think time a part of your daily routine, you not only create greater clarity, purpose and meaning for yourself, but also for your team.

Five Steps That You Can Take Today

1. Evaluate the amount of time you spend thinking about key issues and consider the impact of your decisions.
2. Ask yourself, "Who would benefit if I had a broader range of options to consider?"
3. Use commute time as an opportunity to think deeply about one or two key issues that you currently face.
4. Schedule at least ten minutes of think time on your calendar every day and do your best to honor this commitment by purposefully eliminating distractions.
5. Seek input from your peers and/or team about the importance of think time and solicit feedback about what works well for them.

LEADING THROUGH CHANGE

Ten Strategies for Keeping Your Team Engaged During Times of Change

Like most leaders today, the demands of your job probably require you to multitask at a level never experienced before. The old adage "do more with less" has, in many organizations, been replaced with *do whatever it takes and then some.* To be sure, the constantly accelerating pace of change is at an all-time high in nearly every organization. Not surprisingly, conventional thinking across industries concludes that it's not going to slow anytime soon. Despite this workplace reality and its related challenges, leaders at all levels must ensure a consistently high level of employee engagement during times of change. It is within this context that the following leadership strategies are presented.

1. Do your best to stay positive. As a leader and role model, you set the tone for your team and, in many ways, your organization too. Everything you do or don't do impacts employee engagement at some level.
2. Communicate clearly and frequently. Absent clarity from you and your leadership colleagues, your employees may just feed the rumor mill. At the very least, they will be less likely to understand their role in the change equation. Key questions that nearly all employees need answers to during organizational change include, "What's happening," "Why is it happening," and "How do we need to respond."

3. Stay connected to your team. Despite having to juggle more priorities than ever before, your team still needs you to be there for them. Schedule twenty to thirty minutes of Leadership By Walking Around (LBWA) time on your calendar every week to let your team know that you're there for them and that you care about how they're doing.

4. Limit the amount of closed door time. Although you may need uninterrupted time more frequently than before, the negative perception that closed doors create can add to the stress level of your team while also adding fodder to the rumor mill.

5. Help employees access development resources. Every employee goes through the change process in their own way and in their own time. As such, some employees need more help than others. Whether it's training, employee assistance program (EAP), or some other internal resource, offer support to those employees who struggle with organizational change.

6. Hold periodic "how are you/we" doing discussions with staff. Despite the fact that everyone is multitasking at a very high level, you still need to take the time to assess how your team is making their way through the change process. These periodic discussions can also help to define barriers that you need to remove for your team.

7. Learn to be okay with not having all of the answers. Because of the wide range of factors driving change in today's workplace, uncertainty at one level or another can be expected. Part of being an authentic leader is acknowledging that, at times, you don't have all the answers. Accept this as both okay and quite normal.

8. Challenge employees to find the upside of change. Although it's often easy to focus on the negative impact of change, the truth is that, in most cases, change offers opportunities to

increase the value and impact of everyone's role. Reminding your team that they have found solutions in the past and that you believe in them can go a long way in helping them to discover the silver lining.

9. Hold everyone accountable for team success. Without exception, the success of any change initiative requires that everyone does their part. Aligning talent capacity with interest, needs, and motivation often allows each team member to understand their contribution to team and organizational success.

10. Celebrate even small successes along the way. Every member of your team, regardless of where they are in the change process, enjoys the sweet taste of success. Acknowledging efforts and impact is a powerful mechanism for building motivation and momentum toward desired outcomes.

The constantly accelerating pace of change is at an all-time high in nearly every organization. Not surprisingly, conventional thinking across industries concludes that it's not going to slow anytime soon.

STRESS MANAGEMENT AS A
LEADERSHIP OPPORTUNITY

Ten Strategies for Leading Through Stress

"To whom much is given, much is expected." Although this age-old adage can be attributed to a variety of sources, one thing that is certain is that it is a poignant reminder for all of us who are called to lead in the twenty-first century.

At a foundational level, leadership is a gift and a huge responsibility, which must be honored. After all, who else is provided with countless opportunities each day to influence and impact people's lives in so many ways? While the responsibilities are many and at times burdensome, we must never lose sight of these opportunities nor take them for granted.

One of the most pressing challenges facing leaders today is the accelerating pace of change and the constant drive to do more with less. Add to this the uncertainty of the global economy and its resulting fallout and most workplaces today are experiencing an unparalleled level of stress and anxiety.

To be sure, there are huge bodies of research available on the impact of workplace stress today. Much of which offer a compelling case for why organizations of all types need to address this near epidemic. However, a much smaller body of work has been written about the leader's role in managing stress.

When we consider the wide scope and resulting impact of our influence, we begin to grasp the importance of our role in managing workplace stress. Although as leaders we often must endure a broader range of stress factors, we are obligated to be role models of the behaviors that drive team and organizational success. It is within this context that we begin to discover the opportunity.

Ten Steps You Can Take Now to Turn Stress into a Leadership Opportunity

1. Consider how you manage stress and what impact it has on team engagement and overall morale.
2. Initiate a conversation with your team or peer group about how they manage stress in a healthy and effective way.
3. Invest five minutes to complete the free Workplace Stress Management Inventory on the WorkChoice Solutions web site at www.workchoicesolutions.com. Key words: *learning resources, leadership assessments.*
4. Identify one development opportunity related to your stress management inventory results and map out a series of small, doable steps that you will take between now and year-end.
5. Seek input from your team and other key stakeholders about the range of role model opportunities that are presented during times of stress. Also identify the key behaviors that support being a positive role model in each scenario.
6. Using a scale of one to ten, with one being the equivalent of a minor hassle, and ten being a true catastrophe, assign a number to whatever it is that's making you feel anxious. You'll find that most problems we encounter rate somewhere in the one to five range—in other words, they're really not such a big deal.
7. Create an affirmation or personal mantra. A short, clear, and positive statement that focuses on your coping abilities can be very powerful. Affirmations are a good way to silence the negative self-talk voice we all carry with us that only adds to our stress. The next time you feel as if your life is one

disaster after another, repeat ten times, "I feel calm. I can handle this."

8. Practice mindfulness. Heighten your awareness of the moment by focusing intently on an object. Notice a pencil's shape, color, weight, and feel. Or slowly savor a raisin or a piece of chocolate. Mindfulness leads to relaxation.

9. Just say no. Trying to do everything is a one-way ticket to serious stress. Be clear about your limits and stop trying to please everyone all the time.

10. Ask for help. Effective stress management involves awareness, taking responsibility, choices, action, and commitment. Sometimes it requires external resources too, so don't be afraid to seek help when necessary. All of the important people in your life are counting on you.

One of the most pressing challenges facing leaders today is the accelerating pace of change and the constant drive to do more with less. Add to this the uncertainty of the global economy and its resulting fallout and most workplaces today are experiencing an unparalleled level of stress and anxiety.

THE THREE DIMENSIONS
OF LEADERSHIP TRUST

The list of high priority issues confronting most leaders today is by all accounts long and growing. Competition, return on investment (ROI), stakeholder value, revenue growth, employee engagement, talent management, acquisitions, and on and on the list goes. While all of these and more are very real in most organizations, the common denominator influencing a successful response may very well be trust. Leadership trust to be specific. Sure there are other factors at play here, but absent trust in your leadership, your capacity to turn these "front burner" issues into opportunities may be limited.

As a beginning point, consider your greatest success of the past year. Was it possible to achieve this success without others? More than likely it was not. There were no doubt a wide range of people who played a supporting role in your success. Your team, peers, boss, customers, vendors, and possibly your board too. Trust is the vital element that allows two or more people who work together to know that they can rely on each other implicitly. It is in no small way the driver of collaboration and synergy at its deepest and most powerful level.

Today's changing landscape of work coupled with the overall state of the economy has created both a need and an opportunity for leaders to examine the power of trust and its countless rewards.

To be sure, there are as many definitions or interpretations of the word *trust* as there are people on your team or in your organization. In an effort to build clarity and a framework for consideration, I present what I refer to as the three dimensions of leadership trust.

The first dimension encompasses trust in your skill and capacity to achieve success in your specific role. In this dimension, all of your stakeholders trust that you not only know what you're doing, but also that you know where you're going and how you're going to get there. Even more than this, they trust that it's the right direction.

The second dimension of trust encompasses character. In this dimension, your stakeholders trust that everything you do is done with integrity and consistency and that your actions are aligned with the greater good of the organization. This dimension, by my estimation, may be the most important as character and integrity represent fundamental elements of true leadership. Beyond these factors, your stakeholders trust that you honor your commitments by consistently doing what you say you will do.

A third dimension that warrants consideration is leadership intention. In this dimension, your stakeholders trust that all that you do is not just good for the organization, but also good for each member of the team. It is often that unspoken support that you give to your team that assures them that you are in their corner, doing what it takes to help them succeed. It also encompasses fairness and transparency too. Like leadership character, leadership intention often serves as a guidepost for not only finding the path to true leadership, but also being able to stay there.

Building and maintaining your leadership trust capacity is no small task. It is by all accounts a worthy goal that must be pursued with clarity and purpose. Truly investing the time to explore the impact of your leadership trust may very well be the first step in not only making sense of your "front burner" issues, but also being able to tackle the list with a clear outcome in sight.

Today's changing landscape of work coupled with the overall state of the economy has created both a need and an opportunity for leaders to examine the power of trust and its countless rewards.

Five More Steps You Can Take Now

1. Give yourself permission to take a ten-minute "time-out" from your hectic schedule and consider how the three dimensions apply to you in your role as a leader.
2. Initiate a conversation with your peer group or a trusted mentor about the scope and impact of leadership trust and its connection to employee engagement and organizational success.
3. Try to identify other dimensions of leadership trust and look for their connection to leadership excellence.
4. Seek input from your team and other key stakeholders about what leadership trust means to them and look for ways to expand your leadership trust capacity.
5. Invest three minutes to complete the free *Leadership Trust Inventory* found on the WorkChoice Solutions web site at www.workchoicesolutions.com. Key words: *learning resources, leadership assessments.*

EXPANDING YOUR EMPLOYEE
DEVELOPMENT CAPACITY

One of my favorite *Dilbert* cartoons features the fictional character Alice who is instructed by her "pointy haired" boss to write a performance review of herself for him to sign. Alice asks, "What will our seven layers of management be doing while I manage myself?" Responding to the angry look on her boss's face, she adds, "Sorry, I'll ding myself for that on my evaluation." Her boss then replies, "If you can't find me, have Carol, my secretary, sign my name on your performance review."

While there is certainly some humor to be found in this and other Dilbert cartoons, there is nothing funny about skirting one of leadership's most critical responsibilities, namely employee development discussions. All too often these discussions get relegated to the dreaded once-a-year routine where little benefit actually occurs. I remember a recent coaching case where, early in the project assessment phase, the HR vice president told me that "Bob's issue had been going on for nearly two years." When I asked about Bob's perception of "the issue," I was told that he didn't have a clue because no one had ever told him about "the issue." This may come as a surprise to you, but I have seen this scenario play out more times than I care to remember. The real shocker in many of these cases is that not only does the person not get to hear about "the issue," they go on getting average or above average performance ratings and even bonuses despite the fact that their behavior or lack of results are creating "an issue."

One of the reasons the above scenario plays out with some degree of frequency is that many leaders view employee coaching and development as a complex and time-consuming process. It's not, or at least, it doesn't have to be. Building the case for employee coaching and development begins with acknowledging that this is a critical part of good leadership. It also helps to understand that good leadership is, among other things, about creating more leaders and not more followers. Another reality today is that many world-class organizations have clearly defined performance metrics for leaders that are linked to employee development. Regardless of the motivation, it makes good business sense for leaders to develop meaningful strategies for expanding their coaching capacity.

Often, leaders get distracted by the misconception that they need to be therapists or counselors to be effective with employee coaching and development. This is not the case.

What does help, however, is an open and honest approach that is genuinely supportive of the employee's success. It also helps to recognize that all employees have development needs, not just the poor performers.

There are many scenarios in which a coaching discussion is relevant. Some potential examples include personal enrichment, professional development, performance improvement, and career advancement. In the personal enrichment scenario, the employee may want to expand his or her knowledge of an area that will help them in their role in an indirect way. It may involve learning a new language or even taking a course related to a hobby. In both the professional development and performance improvement scenarios, it is most likely related to helping them to expand their impact in their current job. The career advancement scenario often is linked to their long-term career goals beyond their current role. Regardless of the scenario, it is important to follow a process that moves the employee in the right

> *"Regardless of the scenario, it is important to follow a process that moves the employee in the right direction."*

direction. It is also important to remember that all of the above scenarios encompass learning.

The following is a five-stage process that I have used with many leaders to expand their capacity to coach and develop their employees.

Stage 1: Identify the issue—*what, why, how* and *when* are key questions to consider.

Stage 2: Establish agreement that the issue exists and has consequences if applicable.

Stage 3: Explore and define appropriate solutions, related actions, and metrics.

Stage 4: Provide follow-up support and monitor progress.

Stage 5: Acknowledge progress and success.

While there are other coaching methodologies that you can follow, the above represents an effective process for helping to make sense of your *employee development* leadership responsibility. More importantly, it provides a workable framework for achieving a higher level of employee productivity and engagement.

Five More Steps You Can Take Now

1. Initiate a discussion with your leadership peer group about their view and experiences related to employee coaching and look to expand your own coaching comfort level and capacity.

2. Seek out your HR team for help with the coaching process and work to engage them as your partners in employee development.

3. Identify your bottom three performers and explore what can be done in a collaborative way to help improve their value and impact through a coaching intervention.

4. Identify one key employee who would benefit from a coaching and development discussion and who would allow you to build on your coaching capacity.
5. Invest five minutes to complete the free, Coaching Effectiveness Survey on the WorkChoice Solutions web site. Key words: *learning resources, leadership assessments.*

Rethinking Group Decision-Making

The value of effective group decision-making has been known for a long time. Yet with few exceptions, most leaders and teams today fall short of recognizing the full range of benefits associated with participatory decision-making. All too often, the fastest thinkers or most vocal among the team drive to a decision point that at the least leaves many valuable insights or perspectives off the table. At its most damaging level, others are left wondering why they even attempted to offer their opinion. To be sure, these scenarios play out countless times every day and, in their wake, are capable team members whose motivation may well be diminished.

As a beginning point, it helps to acknowledge that the best decisions are those that reflect the diverse perspectives of the entire group and ultimately the best outcome for all involved.

To a large degree, the barriers that exist within effective group decision-making can be linked to the *do-more-with-less* cultural dynamics that are prevalent in today's workplace. With high productivity a daily expectation, most leaders (and teams) put more emphasis on reaching a conclusion or "getting it done" than they do on making meaningful and inclusive decisions. Despite good intentions, some team members make biased judgments that inhibit a free flow of ideas while also discouraging others from sharing how they really feel or think about an issue.

Another by-product of today's workplace cultural dynamic is the unwritten norms that allow mixed messages to further dilute the group decision-making process. "Tell it like it is, but don't hurt anyone's feelings," "Be well prepared but don't ask too many questions," and perhaps my favorite, "Everyone deserves our attention, but it's okay to check your Blackberry while someone else is speaking."

While much of the above is true for many leaders and teams today, the good news is that with deliberate effort, the full benefit of participatory decision-making can be realized. As a beginning point, it helps to acknowledge that the best decisions are those that reflect the diverse perspectives of the entire group and ultimately the best outcome for all involved. Acknowledging that people often support what they help to create is another important guidepost for leaders and teams.

In addition to being mindful of these group decision-making truths, leaders are well served by also considering the core tenets of participatory decision-making. Not surprisingly, full participation and mutual understanding are the foundational building blocks of effective group decision-making. Inclusiveness where decisions reflect everyone's perspective and truth is another important building block. While these building blocks go a long way in ensuring optimum decisions, shared responsibility for long-term success is paramount. Absent this level of ownership in long-term success, even the best decisions can fall short on the road to implementation.

Five More Steps You Can Take Now

1. Invest the time to consider the effectiveness level of group decision-making within your team and organization. Could it be more effective?
2. Solicit input from your peers and team regarding what they view as the biggest impediments to participatory decision-making.

3. Invest fifteen minutes in your next staff meeting to explore the four core tenets of participatory decision-making and ask your team to define the behaviors that support each tenet.

4. Focus on your short-term goals and small steps toward improving group decision-making with your team and peer group. Remember, small steps are better than no steps.

5. Monitor progress by seeking team feedback following key decisions to ensure that the participatory decision-making process is evolving to a more effective level.

WORKPLACE COMMUNICATIONS

Old Challenges, New Opportunities

J. Edgar Hoover, the esteemed but often controversial head of the FBI who served under several different presidents, was once surprised to discover a rather dramatic increase in FBI activity along the Canadian and Mexican borders. When the FBI director investigated, he found the problem. It turned out that a month or so earlier, Hoover's secretary had asked him to review one of the memos she had typed for him. She wanted him to correct any errors before she sent the memo out to FBI field offices. When Hoover finished his edits, he observed that the margins of the note were much too wide. So he wrote "watch the borders" at the bottom of the memo and gave it back to his secretary to fix and distribute. She logically assumed that Hoover's "watch the borders" comment related to some intelligence alert that he wanted distributed to his FBI border patrols.

While it is unlikely that a communication error of such magnitude would occur in corporate life today, the likelihood that our written and verbal communications are at times misinterpreted remains a very real obstacle in achieving our business objectives. Often, what we say and what is heard is amazingly different. In fact, interpersonal communication skills remain high on the list of desired competencies for workplace success. Therefore, it is no wonder that the issue of workplace communication effectiveness takes center stage in companies from Boston to Bangkok.

Workplace communication can be easy but requires great care and planning with customers, peers, and other coworkers. One of the most important elements of planning is seeking to be a good listener. Knowing your communication goals and desired outcomes is a critical piece of the planning puzzle. However, without a strong desire and commitment to be an active listener, your communication goals and outcomes may not be fully achieved.

Understanding that most people want to be heard more than they want you to agree with them is a good foundation for achieving your communication goals. Many people complain about not being heard, yet they rarely take the time to listen to others.

Despite the many challenges of communicating effectively, good communication skills can be learned. The following are some suggestions for improving your workplace communication effectiveness and impact.

> Workplace communication can be easy but requires great care and planning with customers, peers, and other coworkers. One of the most important elements of planning is seeking to be a good listener. Knowing your communication goals and desired outcomes is a critical piece of the planning puzzle. However, without a strong desire and commitment to be an active listener, your communication goals and outcomes may not be fully achieved.

1. Truly listen and focus on what the other person is saying. Put yourself in "their shoes."
2. Look for common ground. Resist the temptation to focus on differences.
3. Don't interrupt the person. Let them tell their whole story.
4. Restate what you think you heard. Strive for clarity and understanding.
5. Stay positive and be a role model for effective communication. Your goal is to create a win-win every time!

From improving interpersonal relationships to achieving more win-win outcomes, the pursuit of successful communication is worth the effort. We each have an opportunity to increase our communication effectiveness and impact. While the skills required to achieve this goal can be learned, they do not occur without awareness, commitment, and practice. When we communicate effectively, we succeed.

As the range and pace of change accelerate at work and the demands of doing "more with less" become a daily reality, improving the impact of our workplace communications may be the first step in turning old challenges into new opportunities.

The Distraction Epidemic

"The main thing is keeping the main thing, the main thing." This powerful observation from author Steven R. Covey offers a multitude of insights into one of today's most pressing leadership challenges. On one level, it reminds us of the constant need for a keen, unwavering focus on things that matter most. On another level, it offers an inspiring guidepost for helping us to discover our full leadership capacity both in and out of work.

With very few exceptions, leaders today are stretched (and in many cases stressed) to a level that borders on unhealthy. Add to this the accelerating demands of life outside of work and most leaders would agree that it's a huge challenge to keep the main thing, the main thing with a high degree of consistency.

Over the last several months, I have had numerous conversations about this universal leadership challenge with clients and colleagues at all levels and across many industries and sectors. Again and again, I hear that the increased demands of work and life result in leaders and teams feeling distracted at an epidemic level.

It doesn't matter where you work or what you do, you probably deal with a multitude of distractions on a daily basis. And these distractions are costly. A 2010 study by consulting firm Workplace Options estimates that distractions cost US businesses $650 billion per year in lost productivity. The cost may very well be higher if the *less than optimum decision-making* associated with being distracted is factored into the equation.

Not surprisingly, many of today's workplace distractions are driven in one way or another by the pursuit of competitive advantage, higher productivity, or increased profit margins. While none of these factors are unreasonable, they often create a paradox worth considering. Simply put, the distraction by-product of these pursuits can, at times, create an impediment to recognizing these desired outcomes. A further irony is that meaningful success or achievement in any of these pursuits demands that we have a razor-sharp focus on what matters most at all times.

While the business impact remains high, the personal impact may be even higher in large part because leadership excellence applies to all areas or aspects of our lives. Additionally, the stress that often results from being distracted can have far-reaching implications beyond the workplace. By my estimation, the most compelling reason for managing my distractions is that in doing so, I get to spend more time being the leader that I want to be not just at work, but in life too. Another important motivation that most leaders can relate to is that our best work comes from being well-grounded and fully present. Both of which are impossible if we don't deliberately manage our distractions.

What's a leader to do? As a beginning point, it helps to acknowledge that workplace distractions in all of their forms are both a real and an inevitable part of today's do-more-with-less business climate. It might also help to acknowledge that as leaders, we are the role models for the behavior that we expect or desire from others. To be sure, an important part of our work as leaders is to set the right example while helping our teams and ourselves to keep the main thing, the main thing.

> *"The stress that often results from being distracted can have far reaching impact beyond the workplace."*

Ten More Steps You Can Take Now

1. Invest the time to assess the most common distractions in your day and consider ways to limit or minimize your exposure to these distractions.

2. Initiate a conversation with your team to assess their most common distractions and identify actions that you can take to remove or limit their daily distractions.

3. Focus on your short-term goals. Consider why you want to achieve these goals and redirect your attention and energy to getting back on track.

4. Remember your purpose and what truly matters to reduce the distractions and reenergize your focus and motivation.

5. Remember, you have some control over what distracts you. When you refocus your attention to what is in your control and readjust your focus on your goals, the distractions diminish.

6. Schedule e-mail and phone time. Minimize these distractions by scheduling specific times to check and respond to e-mail and phone calls.

7. Take short breaks to clear your mind. Even five minutes away from the distraction can help you to refocus and prioritize.

8. Talk to interrupters. Consider having a candid conversation with habitual interrupters about the impact they have on your daily productivity.

9. Resist the urge to allow distractions to put you in the panic mode.

10. Invest ten minutes to consider "the main thing" in all of your roles as a leader.

THE KINDNESS CONNECTION

As a passionate student of leadership, I have had the good fortune of being able to learn from many leaders over the years. While experience continues to be a trusted teacher, my countless conversations with leaders at all levels have proven to be an invaluable source of knowledge and inspiration. A common thread woven through every conversation is the exploration of how leadership has evolved *and* what separates great leaders from all of the rest.

To be sure, timeless factors such as integrity, trust, respect, consistency, and transparency continue to serve as the foundational building blocks of leadership excellence. Although these factors remain at the core of leadership effectiveness, today's complex work climate coupled with the accelerating pace of global change demand more from us as leaders. Central to this demand by my estimation and by the estimation of many leaders I've spoken with is the need for a higher level of kindness not just at work but outside of work too. One executive I spoke with recently summed it up quite well when she said, "Today's kindness deficit has resulted in countless people and organizations being emotionally bankrupt. People are hungry for kindness, and as leaders, we must honor our responsibility as role models."

As a beginning point, kindness is a part of what great leaders do not just occasionally, but also consistently. Highly effective leaders know that kindness reduces the emotional distance between two people and, as a result, creates a human connection. At another significant level, kindness allows us to forge deeper human bonds, which not surprisingly are key to collaboration and a sense of belonging. When we are kind to each other, new relationships are formed, and existing relationships are strengthened.

Much has been written about the positive impact of kindness, and while many studies point to related health benefits, the greater motivation for today's successful leader is that kindness is contagious. Few people are immune to the emotional impact of kindness and, as a result, are often inspired to "pay it forward." Imagine for a moment the last time that someone was kind to you. Was it possible that you extended an act of kindness to someone else? More than likely you did, and the resulting impact not only created a human connection, but also made you feel good too.

I remember a dear mentor friend of mine who summed up his motivation for being kind as simply, "It feels nice to be nice." When we are kind to others, it is nearly impossible not to feel the emotional warmth that kindness produces in ourselves and in others.

Being kind goes well beyond a new demand of leadership. It is one of the great opportunities afforded to all leaders regardless of job title or number of direct reports. Not surprisingly, it is an opportunity afforded to everyone not just at work, but outside of work too.

As we make our way through the ever-increasing demands of our busy lives, let us be mindful of the countless opportunities we are given to discover the kindness connection.

> *"Today's kindness deficit has resulted in countless people and organizations being emotionally bankrupt. People are hungry for kindness, and as leaders, we must honor our responsibility as role models."*

Ten Things You Can Do Today

1. Give the gift of nonjudgmental listening to one person.
2. Choose to be fully present when speaking with a member of your team or family.
3. Say thank you two more times today than you did yesterday.
4. Tell someone that they are important to you.

5. Offer an honest compliment to a stranger, a friend, or member of your team.

6. Send a thank-you note to one person who has been kind to you.

7. Write a positive, affirming e-mail to a member of your team or other coworker.

8. Allow another driver the right of way at a stop sign or stoplight on your way home.

9. Offer to help a friend in need—even a few minutes of your time can make a difference.

10. Acknowledge a complete stranger with a smile.

Bridging the Engagement Gap

Eight No-Cost Strategies for Increasing Employee Engagement

Despite the efforts of many well-intentioned leaders, the gap between engaged employees and disengaged employees continues to grow. Numerous studies have confirmed that regardless of industry, market sector, or organizational size, the ratio of disengaged employees to engaged employees remains at nearly 3 to 1. While this number at first glance is quite unsettling, the good news is that not all of the disengaged employees are fully disenfranchised or disconnected. Some (or possibly many) are what are best described as ambivalent. These employees struggle to understand where they fit in the organization and perhaps, even more importantly, what the future holds for them. To be sure, the struggle for engagement most often arises from a longing to be more than their job, to feel connected to and proud of the organization of which they are a part.

This universal desire represents the common ground shared by engaged and disengaged employees alike and offers leaders the opportunity to reengage the ambivalent and maybe even the disengaged too.

How do astute leaders who understand the relationship between engagement and results do this? The answer is really very simple: they satisfy those universal desires. They help employees become more than their jobs, feel connected to, and proud of the organization. The following eight no-cost strategies will not only help to bridge the engagement gap, but also quite possibly help leaders move from well-intentioned to highly effective.

1. Assess your leadership. As a leader, you set the tone for your team. Everything you do or don't do impacts employee engagement at some level. How well do you model the behavior you want from your team? Do you demonstrate the critical leadership characteristics of openness, integrity, resilience, trust, and respect? What are the top five characteristics of your leadership style and what impact do they have on your team?

2. Show employees that you value them. Research shows that one of the chief influencers of motivation and engagement is feeling valued. You don't need a complex program to show employees you value them. Connecting with people on a personal level and building relationships can take you much further. Schedule twenty to thirty minutes of Leadership By Walking Around time on your calendar every week to let your team know that you're there for them and that you care about how they're doing.

3. Communicate clearly and frequently. Another key factor in engagement is providing information that enables them to do their job and information about what is happening in the organization, especially around change. Keep them informed about what is happening and why it is happening and its impact on the team so they don't have to depend on the rumor mill.

4. Ensure performance expectations are clear and attainable. Develop specific measures by soliciting input from employees. Hold everyone accountable for team success. Aligning talent capacity with interest, needs and

> *"These employees struggle to understand where they fit in the organization and perhaps, even more importantly, what the future holds for them."*

motivation allows each team member to understand their contribution to team and organizational success.

5. Link each person's role and contribution to the key goals of the department and organization. The more each employee understands how their efforts impact the greater good of the group, the more likely they are to find meaning in their work.

6. Give timely and specific feedback. No one knowingly chooses to fail. People need feedback in order to improve their performance. Make sure your feedback helps and motivates them to improve.

7. Involve employees. Hold a discussion with your team about their view of engagement and what they think are the key actions and behaviors that support success for the group and organization. Identify the top three shared motivation drivers of the group. Involving them helps to build a common language, clarify purpose, and increase their ownership.

8. Manage the rumor mill. Play an active role in managing your team's perception of the organization. Focus on what is working well and on the positive aspects of the culture including recent successes, external reputation, shared values, and future goals. Above all, never contribute to the rumor mill no matter how tempting it may be.

Deliberate Leadership in a Distracted World

Although I have been fortunate to discover many leadership truths over the last twenty-five years, one truth continues to have the most far-reaching benefit in my life. To be sure, there are numerous leadership lessons that have served me well, but all of them combined don't equal the cumulative power of believing that there is no *off switch* on leadership. The truth is that everyone of us can demonstrate leadership in every role we play, not just at work, but everywhere, every day.

While most leaders would be quick to acknowledge the opportunity this truth presents, most would also agree that it's a challenge to seize the opportunity at every juncture. Despite the fact that real leadership is so desperately needed in all corners of our society today, the multitude of distractions we face often prevent us from not only seeing the opportunity, but also seizing it too.

The National Science Foundation and other prestigious research organizations have confirmed that on average, our brains produce anywhere from thirty-five thousand to fifty thousand thoughts each day. Add to this the accelerating drive for enhanced productivity and the dizzying array of technology available to us, and it's no wonder that we are distracted at a near epic level.

The truth is that we live in an increasingly distracted world where it is difficult to focus on any one thought for more than a few seconds before new distractions arise. While the implications of this truth are many, the most significant may very well be its impact on our capacity to seize the leadership opportunity with clarity and consistency. Absent a deliberate, focused effort to manage our daily distractions, we simply cannot expect to be highly effective leaders in any of our roles.

Like the word *leadership*, the word *deliberate* means different things to different people. At a foundational level, *deliberate* is the absence of being impulsive or hurried. In many ways it is the opposite of distracted in that it allows us to be far more purposeful in whatever action we take. Being purposeful not only affords us a better range of decision-making possibilities, but also allows us to lead more often and in more places.

Several years ago, I had the realization that like most people I knew, my life was a series of one distraction after another from the moment I awoke each day. Knowing that this had the potential to prevent me from spending most of my waking hours on the leadership path, I decided that I had to manage it in a more proactive way. What followed was a combination of divine intervention, and more than likely, the wisdom of a few dear friends.

For as long as I can remember, I had started my day with a few minutes of quiet time and self-reflection. Most of which was focused on building my to-do list for the day. I still invest the time to do my daily to-do list, but my morning routine has taken on a far more deliberate dimension.

Every morning of every day, I devote at least twenty minutes to what I call my compass calibration time. In this quiet space, I reflect on three questions. The first is, "What's important to me today?" This question allows me to reconnect to my moral compass and associated values. It reminds me of who I am and what I stand for. The second question is, "Why are these things important to me?" Beyond allowing me to connect more deeply to my core values, this question allows me to connect to my true purpose. Finally, I explore the third question, which is, "How do I need to show up in all of my roles today?" This question not only allows me to have far more clarity around my behavior, but, in doing so, also fosters leadership congruence across every role I play that day.

Is it easy and convenient to do this every day? Of course not. I find myself struggling with it at times and occasionally am so distracted that I have a hard time focusing on all three questions. In fact, some days it takes me the full twenty minutes just to quiet my mind. What follows however is far more clarity and the capacity to manage my daily distractions in a deliberate way.

Ten More Things You Can Do Now

1. Invest the time to assess the most common distractions in your day and consider ways to limit or minimize your exposure to these distractions.
2. Calibrate your compass every morning through deliberate meditation, prayer, or self-reflection.
3. Make an effort to slow down or shut off the "auto pilot" more frequently.
4. Initiate a conversation with your team to assess their most common distractions and identify actions that you can take to remove or limit their daily distractions.
5. Focus on your short-term goals. Consider why you want to achieve these goals and redirect your attention and energy to getting back on track.
6. Remember your purpose and what truly matters to reduce the distractions and reenergize your focus and motivation.
7. Take short breaks to clear your mind. Even five minutes away from the distraction can help you to refocus and prioritize.
8. Utilize a daily affirmation or mantra to help stay grounded.
9. Resist the urge to allow distractions to put you in the panic mode.
10. Remember, you have some control over what distracts you. When you refocus your attention to what is in your control and readjust your focus on your goals, the distractions diminish.

Building an

Accountability Mindset

With very few exceptions, most leaders today would be quick to acknowledge that their teams could be more engaged. Not surprisingly, many would also readily admit that they have made more than a few attempts to boost team engagement, often times with only minimal impact. To be sure, boosting employee engagement requires far more than a single initiative or program. Well respected research from such giants as Gallup, Mercer and Blessing White confirm that sustainable increases in employee engagement require among other things; executive buy-in, leadership clarity and a systematic approach that holds everyone accountable for engagement.

While much has been written about the systematic approach to bolstering engagement, the resulting tidal wave of data and complex solutions often result in an engagement paralysis for some leaders and organizations. Add to this the rapid pace of change and the overall white-water pace of business today and it's no wonder that many well-intentioned engagement initiatives have fallen flat on the road to implementation.

At the root of engagement is a personal accountability mindset which acknowledges that doing a job well and with a good attitude is not only a reasonable organizational expectation, but also one that enhances job satisfaction. At an even deeper level, personal accountability involves a range of behaviors that despite rapid change, ambiguity or even full buy-in, allows the individual to view their role as an integral part of the organization's success. Helping employees to see their role in this light not only creates greater ownership and accountability but also increased purpose and motivation, both drivers of engagement.

While writing my first book, I uncovered many insights about personal accountability and the behaviors that encompass a personal accountability mindset. Through multiple conversations with teams and leaders, I identified 10 core behaviors that encompass the personal accountability mindset. They include:

1. Accepts responsibility for own performance, success and development.
2. Displays confidence in decisions and commitments, even under pressure.
3. Is proactive in demonstrating initiative and in honoring commitments.
4. Takes responsibility for knowing what's expected of them.
5. Focuses on finding solutions more than finding problems.
6. Demonstrates energy and persistence in tackling challenging assignments.
7. Supports leadership directives even when not in full agreement.
8. Encourages co-workers to excel in their work and lends support when needed.
9. Takes pride in doing good work and in being a positive role model.
10. Never contributes to the rumor mill.

Another important leadership insight that surfaced in my accountability conversations was that due to the leader's vast range of influence, they need to consistently demonstrate a very high level of accountability. I also came to believe that a key differentiator between high performing organizations and others is a culture of accountability where all employees demonstrate an accountability mindset.

What is an accountability mindset? Simply put, it's a belief shared by all employees (regardless of level or title) that others are counting on us to go the extra mile to achieve a quality outcome. Said another way, it's an acceptance of the obligation (and opportunity) to do more than is expected well and with a good attitude.

There are many factors that inhibit the accountability mindset but chief among them is lack of clarity about employer expectations. A dozen years ago when I was writing my first book, I remember uncovering a powerful truth about employee accountability and engagement that is still relevant today. Specifically, *no employee regardless of level or personality type ever intentionally shows up at work with a desire to fail.* I've discussed this truth with more leaders than I can possibly count and despite the occasional pushback statement such as, "you haven't met _____", most people believe this fundamental truth. The belief that there are exceptions to this maxim is often an attempt to excuse failed leadership.

Clarity of expectations is not only a key driver of an accountability mindset but also a basic human motivator. Although clarifying expectations is often seen as a leadership responsibility, the reality is that this task is everyone's responsibility. Despite this, as leaders we need to ensure that all employees can easily answer such questions as;

- What are my key deliverables?
- Who am I responsible to?
- What is their desired outcome?
- What are my key timelines and milestones?
- What resources are available to assist me?
- Am I absolutely clear on what's expected of me?

Your team's capacity to answer these questions with ease will impact their attainment of desired outcomes. Teams must also fully understand what behaviors are expected of them.

In my work with leaders and teams all over the country, I continue to be struck by the lack of clarity that teams have about acceptable and unacceptable behavior. Sure there are many well written employee handbooks chock full of policies but all too often, few employees can readily identify the behaviors that support or inhibit team and organizational success. Without this understanding, most leaders and teams are at a disadvantage.

Creating clarity around behavioral expectations is not a complicated or cumbersome endeavor. Marvin Weisbord in his excellent book, Productive Workplaces Revisited, (Jossey-Bass Publishing) reminds us that "people support what they help to create." By investing the time to define a shared set of behaviors that drive team and organizational success, you not only help to build an accountability mindset but also a roadmap for bringing out the best in every member of your team.

7 More Steps You Can Take Now to Build An Accountability Mindset:

1. Assess your leadership. As a leader, you set the climate for your team. Everything you do or don't do impacts employee accountability and engagement at some level. How well do you model the behavior you want from your team? Do you demonstrate the critical leadership characteristics of openness, integrity, resilience, trust, and respect? What are the top five characteristics of your leadership style and what impact do they have on your team and their level of accountability?

2. Involve employees. Solicit input from your team about their view of accountability and what they think are the key actions that embody an accountability mindset. Also ask them to consider the actions and behaviors that inhibit an accountability mindset. Identify the top 5 accountability behaviors that drive team success. Involving your team helps to build a common language, clarify purpose and increase their ownership.

3. Show employees that you value them. Research shows that one of the chief influencers of motivation and engagement is feeling valued. You don't need a complex program to

show employees that you value them. Schedule 20 minutes of Leadership By Walking Around time on your calendar every week to let your team know that you're there for them and that you care about how they're doing.

4. Communicate clearly and frequently. Another key factor in building an accountability mindset is keeping your team informed about what is happening in the organization, especially around change. Beyond helping them to do their job with greater clarity and purpose, clear and frequent communication from you goes a long way in reducing or even eliminating the rumor mill.

5. Link each person's role and contribution to the key goals of the organization. The more employees understand how their efforts impact the greater good of the group, the more likely they are to help foster an accountability mindset.

6. Give timely and specific feedback. No one knowingly chooses to fail. People need feedback in order to improve their performance. Make sure your feedback helps and motivates them to improve while also reinforcing the accountability mindset behaviors.

7. Emphasize continuous improvement. Acknowledge that personal leadership and the accountability mindset is part of a learning continuum that through time and commitment allows us to achieve greater job impact and greater job satisfaction. Encourage your team to complete the Navigator Inventory 2.0 assessment to help create a development baseline while also helping to build greater clarity around the accountability mindset behaviors. Visit www.workchoicesolutions.com key words, Learning Resources, Leadership Assessments to access and complete the assessment.

The 5% Formula

Father's Day reminded me of the many lessons I learned from my dad, and my decision to dedicate my first book to him was easy. Beyond being a terrific father, he was the most decent, patient and selfless person I have ever met. Although I've been fortunate to have many leadership heroes over my career, he remains at the top of the list. Everything he did was about allowing his moral compass to guide him. He was a Master Navigator for sure. He was also a deeply religious and principled man. He didn't say much but when he did, it was always kind, respectful and meaningful.

Earlier in my career and shortly after my second promotion to the leadership ranks, I remember asking my dad about his leadership success formula. He had enjoyed a distinguished 40 year career in law enforcement and had retired as one of the most senior leaders of his agency. He was a highly successful and well respected professional by all accounts. His answer to my success formula inquiry was quite powerful in its simplicity. He was quick to say that a lot of things had influenced his success over the years but one thing that stood out for him was his 5% Formula.

His 5% Formula he went on to tell me, was about always giving 5% more than people expect. He had worked with a lot of people over 40 years and had certainly observed a wide range of successful people over that timeframe. He said he was lucky to learn this early in his career and as a result, made this one of his important guideposts along the way. He went on to say that it had been his observation over much of his career that very few people actually give 100% of themselves to their work. In fact, he didn't think that giving 100% was realistic. "The best you can do is exceed their expectations" he said. Sometimes that takes 80% of your effort and other times it takes 90% of your effort but it always takes 5% more than they expect.

Although my dad's success formula was quite relevant when I first heard it, I think it's even more relevant today. With very few exceptions, every leader I know is faced with the daily challenge of building or maintaining high levels of employee engagement. To be sure, engagement is the engine that drives high performance and your leadership is the fuel that makes engagement possible.

Giving 5% more than is expected in any area of your life, be it work or family or friends goes a long way in a creating a higher level of success and satisfaction. It also represents a powerful example for your team as you lead them through the rapidly changing landscape of today's workplace.

Five More Steps You Can Take Now:

1. Engage your team in a conversation about what the 5%Formula means to them. Consider asking them to define what role the 5% Formula plays in team success and job satisfaction.

2. Initiate a conversation with your leadership peer group to assess how the 5% Formula applies to you as a leadership team. Consider asking each peer to identify at least one thing they can do to demonstrate the 5% Formula in any part of their role to help foster greater personal accountability and ownership among team members.

3. Take the time to assess the scope of your leadership influence and consider what impact it has on team engagement and employee satisfaction. Explore ways in which the 5%Formula can be incorporated into your leadership strategy to help expand your leadership influence and impact.

4. Solicit input from your team about the workplace behaviors that embody the 5% Formula. Ask them to identify daily or weekly opportunities within your department or broader organization where they can apply the 5% Formula.

5. Initiate a conversation with other leadership team members about the impact that the 5% Formula has on customer satisfaction, employee morale and financial performance. Commit to including an exploration of the 5% Formula and its link to these factors over an extended period of time. Even 30 minutes per week over 3 to 6 months could have a significant impact on your capacity to make the 5% Formula part of your culture.

Hope, The New Leadership Competency

With performance review season about to get under way in many organizations, countless conversations will be focused on leadership competencies. Despite a wide range of universal competencies that drive leadership success, few of these conversations will include a measure of the leader's capacity to build hope. To be sure, competencies like visioning, execution, resource management and the full list of EI related competencies (to name a few) remain critical measures of leadership impact. What's changed however is that today's workforce is overworked and overstressed to a point where hope has been replaced by uncertainty and fear in many organizations.

As a beginning point, it's helpful to consider what *hope* as a leadership competency involves. At a foundational level, hope is the absence of fear. It is the belief that the future (even tomorrow) offers an improved state of well-being. At another level, hope is the belief that the positive outweighs the negative. Within the context of work, it means that despite our daily challenges, we're going in the right direction and we'll be okay or even better off when we get to where we're going. Herein resides one of the greatest opportunities available to leaders today. Namely, the opportunity to build hope not just as an antidote for fear but even more importantly, as a building block of community, resilience and engagement.

With very few exceptions, employees at every level are subjected to the rumor mill and all of its toxic, fear inducing half-truths. In

25 years of exploring this organizational phenomenon, I have never uncovered a positive or inspiring story that was spun in the rumor mill of organizations large or small. All too often these stories serve to erode trust, collaboration, accountability and of course, hope too.

Several years ago, I introduced the *"good news deficit"* concept as a way of not only helping to manage the rumor mill but also to help gauge the ratio of good news to bad news that employees are exposed to. Although quite simple, the concept and related test received positive feedback from leaders far and wide. In addition to validating my belief that the rumor mill was a very real impediment to employee morale and engagement, the feedback confirmed that the good news deficit was growing.

Take the good news deficit test in your world of work. Simply assess the ratio of organization specific good news to bad news (rumor mill included) that your employees hear or read in the span of one week. More than likely, the good news deficit in your organization is growing too. Creating hope involves more than this but it's an important consideration as you guide your team through and beyond the challenges of today's workplace.

Napoleon Bonaparte once said that "true leaders are dispensers of hope" Clearly, if there was ever a time when your team needed hope it's now. In fact it's probably safe to say that your team is hungry for hope. While there is no single, magic formula for helping teams to move from fear to hope, there is a wide range of leadership strategies that aid in this process. What follows are some leadership actions worth considering.

10 More Steps You Can Take Now:

1. Invest the time to assess the good news deficit in your organization to help gauge the ratio of good news to bad news that employees are exposed to on a weekly basis. Also

consider what impact this ratio has on team morale and engagement.

2. Seek feedback from your team and peer group about the good news deficit at your organization and encourage everyone to share ideas on how to reduce or eliminate the deficit across your organization. Also assess the range and scope of your organization's rumor mill to help identify themes that may need to be addressed in a proactive manner.

3. Initiate a conversation with your leadership peer group to explore each leader's role and strategy for communicating a consistent leadership message within a predetermined schedule or sequence.

4. Assess the frequency and content of your own leadership communications and consider what impact they have on creating hope for your team.

5. Challenge yourself and others to uncover and celebrate positive outcomes and team wins, however small.

6. Consider doing a weekly "round-up" or summary of organizational and team successes that serve to remind everyone of what is working well.

7. Stay connected to your team. Despite having to juggle more priorities than ever before, your team still needs you to be there for them. Schedule 20 minutes of Leadership By Walking Around (LBWA) time on your calendar every week to let your team know that you're there for them and that you care about how they're doing.

8. Look for opportunities to reinforce your vision of the future and how it creates an improved state of well-being for all stakeholders.

9. Resist the urge to allow daily pressures or small setbacks to put you in the fear mode.

10. Remember, your leadership influence is huge and you set the tone. If you project a sense of hope, your team is likely to do the same.

Beyond Engagement

How a New Legacy Mindset Changes Everything

I've been having the leadership legacy conversation with my coaching clients for years. In most cases, these conversations take the form of an exploration of what the leader wants to be known for and of course, what they want to leave behind after they've moved on for one reason or another. Although this process continues to provide significant value for most leaders I work with, I've come to believe that the concept of legacy goes well beyond the realm of leadership. Webster dictionary defines legacy as, "anything handed down from the past, as from an ancestor or predecessor." For many, leaving a legacy is associated with the end of one's career and how their contribution has left things better off for the organization and its stakeholders. While this is important, today's intensely competitive and complex work environment demands a broader view.

With few exceptions, leaders at all levels are keenly aware of how employee engagement drives organizational success. As a result, vast sums of money and other resources are routinely invested in trying to move the engagement needle forward. Despite many well-intentioned efforts toward this end, much of the available data continues to illustrate significant gaps in employee engagement across industries. Struck by this reality, (which has trended in this direction for several years) I have explored the legacy link to engagement within my circle of clients and colleagues. What has resulted from these numerous conversations is not only a new view of legacy, but perhaps more importantly, a leadership framework for moving well beyond engagement as we know it today.

As a beginning point, legacy is not bound by time, age or the stage in a person's career. It's also not limited to a particular level of hierarchy in an organization. Rather, it's the sum of our efforts and commitment (regardless of role) toward improving our workplace and leaving things better off each day. By my estimation, this is the breakthrough thinking that can and should allow leaders and teams to harness a legacy mindset to take engagement to a new level.

Central to this new legacy mindset is the belief that every employee has the capacity to leave things better off each and everyday. To achieve its full benefit, this belief must be shared by everyone, not just by you and your leadership peers. Consider for a moment how things would be different for you as a leader if your team had this level of clarity and purpose. Imagine how your employee engagement numbers would shift. More than likely, the positive shift would fuel an even higher level of job satisfaction too.

To be sure, leading your team to embrace this new legacy mindset may be one of the most demanding endeavors of your leadership journey. It might help to remember that your capacity to develop your team to this level of clarity and purpose may very well be what defines your leadership legacy.

7 Things You Can Do Now to Build A New Legacy Mindset:

1. Invest the time to assess your level of leadership clarity including your core values and beliefs and how they guide your leadership actions and behaviors. Consider how they influence team trust, clarity of expectations and decision making. Also consider how well you role model the behaviors you expect from your team.

2. Initiate a conversation with your leadership peer group about their view of leadership legacy and explore how the new legacy mindset can impact employee engagement and job satisfaction. Also define a set of leadership behaviors that reinforce the new legacy mindset. Solicit input from your HR partners to help refine your leadership strategy relative to both scenarios.

3. Seek feedback from your team about their definition of leadership legacy and then explore how the new legacy mindset definition can be linked to their definition. Also encourage them to develop a list of team behaviors that support and inhibit the new legacy mindset and its impact on team success.

4. Assess the frequency and content of your leadership communications and consider what impact they have on creating a legacy mindset among your team. Be sure to provide positive feedback and reinforcement in real time as appropriate.

5. Consider doing a monthly "round-up" or summary of team successes that serve to remind everyone of how the new legacy mindset is having a positive impact on organizational performance.

6. Link each person's role and contribution to the key goals of the organization. The more employees understand how their efforts impact the greater good of the group, the more likely they are to help foster a new legacy mindset.

7. Look for opportunities to reinforce your leadership legacy vision of the future and how it creates an improved state of well-being for all stakeholders.

BRIDGING THE GENERATIONAL DIVIDE

5 Strategies for Harnessing Team Capacity

"Every generation imagines itself to be more intelligent than the one that went before it, and wiser than the one that comes after it." This observation, attributed to George Orwell offers a multitude of insights into one of today's most pressing organizational challenges. Namely, to get employees from multiple generations to work together toward a shared goal. On one level, it reminds us that the gaps we see in the generational divide are not unique to one generational group nor are they new. In fact, these generational perceptions have been traced all the way back to ancient Greece when Aristotle said, "The young people would always rather do noble deeds than useful ones. Their lives are regulated more by moral feeling than by reasoning."

Orwell's observation also offers a context for tackling one of the biggest obstacles to bridging the generational divide and ultimately, to harnessing the collective talent and capacity of today's multi-generational workforce.

The typical picture that is painted of today's millennial generation (Gen Y) is that of an arrogant, self-absorbed and entitled group who resent authority and who have an unquenchable thirst for feedback and praise. We're also led to believe other broad generalizations such as Millennials are tech wizards and Baby Boomers are tech dinosaurs. The fact remains that this skill spectrum knows no generational boundaries. What we can learn from Orwell's observation and Aristotle's insight is that these less then flattering descriptors can actually be associated with nearly every generation over the course of human history. Unfortunately, we have been sold the idea of this generational divide through countless articles and stories that exacerbate the perceived differences between generational groups by casting them in a negative light.

When left unchallenged, the perceived differences take root and devolve to point where stereotyping is allowed to flourish. The resulting biases not only impede teamwork and collaboration but also further widen the generational divide. To be sure, today's do more with less; intensely competitive work environment mandates teamwork and collaboration at the highest level.

Although differences do exist among the various generational groups, there is a growing body of research that paints a picture of deeply rooted similarities. Chief among them is what each group wants from their employer. What millennials want from their employer is strikingly similar to that of the genxers and Baby Boomers; challenging and meaningful work, fairness, opportunities to learn and advance as well as competitive compensation. Additionally, all three generational groups share a parallel view that an effective leader is a person who leads by example, acts with integrity, creates linkage between role and organizational goals and challenges employees to improve.

With very few exceptions, the topic of generational differences in today's workplace is on the minds of leaders and teams in nearly every industry or sector. While having as many as four generations working together toward a common goal has its challenges, it also represents an unparalleled opportunity for organizations that can harness this diversity to increase team collaboration and impact.

To effectively harness, engage and motivate today's multi-generational workforce, successful organizations must strive to create a culture of mutual understanding, respect and appreciation. To be sure, the differences among each generational group will remain constant just as they have for centuries. By shifting the focus from differences to common ground, talents and shared purpose, you not only enhance collaboration but also take the first step in bridging the generational divide.

5 Things You Can Do Now to Bridge the Generational Divide:

1. Invest the time to assess the cultural norms of your organization as they relate to generational stereotyping. A simple but impactful process would involve asking a random, cross section of your team or organization to generate a list of descriptors for each generational group. Adding an anonymous context to this process will likely produce a very telling picture of the scope of the generational divide among your employees.

2. Initiate a conversation with your leadership peer group about their view of the generational divide and challenge them to explore leadership behaviors that widen the divide as well as those that serve to bridge the divide. Also define a set of leadership behaviors that can be incorporated into a leadership strategy for helping others to appreciate generational differences and talents.

3. Solicit input from your HR partners to help refine your leadership strategy and engage them as co-pilots in helping to build a culture of mutual understanding, respect and appreciation.

4. Seek feedback from your team about their impression of the generational divide and ask them to consider what role they play in widening the divide and bridging the divide. Also encourage them to define the specific talents and attributes that each generational group brings to the team and how these contribute to organizational success.

5. Link each person's role, talents and contribution to the key goals of the organization. The more employees understand how their talents and the talents of their colleagues impact team success, the more likely they will be to cast generational differences in a positive light.

ONE QUESTION THAT MATTERS

With few exceptions, most people would choose job satisfaction over job distress by a wide margin. Although many factors influence job *satisfaction* or *distress*, all are driven by either internal or external factors. To be sure, one of the most common external factors is poor leadership where among other things; employees don't feel respected, valued or significant. While many leaders would agree that there is always room for improvement; they would also agree that internal factors play a significant role in the job *satisfaction* / job *distress* equation.

Like the external factors, there is a wide range of internal factors that influence the degree to which employees derive meaning or frustration from their work. At the core of the internal factors are attitude and behavior, both of which are choices that have tremendous influence on job satisfaction.

When writing my first book, I explored the attitude and behavior link to job satisfaction at a very deep level. One strategy that I shared for expanding awareness about attitude and behavior involved taking stock of your reputation among stakeholders. Do they see you as part of the solution *or* part of the problem? Does your attitude and corresponding behavior support *or* inhibit team success? Would you be the first *or* last person they'd want on a new project? What role do you play in your level of job satisfaction or distress?

While each of these questions can produce valuable insight into the impact of our attitude and behavior, there remains *one question that matters* which embodies all four.

Specifically, **how easy are you to work with?**

Workplace success for the vast majority of people today is driven by the need to collaborate. Increasingly, employees at every level are required to interact with and contribute to the efforts of many stakeholders both in and out of the organization. How that collaboration happens or doesn't happen not only influences our reputation but ultimately, our capacity to use our talents and to derive satisfaction from our work.

Answering the question, **how easy are you to work with** like any worthwhile endeavor takes more than a single effort. Although there are many aspects or dimensions to the question, it's safe to say that at a foundational level, *personal accountability* encompasses most of them.

At the root of personal accountability is a mindset which acknowledges that doing a job well and with a good attitude is not an unreasonable organizational expectation. In truth, it also plays a huge role in job satisfaction and job impact as well.

Over the last 20 years, I have had countless conversations about personal accountability and its link to job satisfaction with employees at every level. The resulting input helped to identify 10 core behaviors that encompass the personal accountability mindset. They include:

1. Accepts responsibility for own performance, success and development.
2. Displays confidence in decisions and commitments, even under pressure.
3. Is proactive in demonstrating initiative and in honoring commitments.
4. Takes responsibility for knowing what's expected of them.
5. Focuses on finding solutions more than finding problems.
6. Demonstrates energy and persistence in tackling challenging assignments.
7. Supports leadership directives even when not in full agreement.

8. Encourages co-workers to excel in their work and lends support when needed.
9. Takes pride in doing good work and in being a positive role model.
10. Never contributes to the rumor mill.

Taking the time to consider how you model or don't model these accountability behaviors may be the first step in fully grasping the scope of the **how easy are you to work with** question. Not surprisingly, there is a direct correlation between your answer to this question and the level of satisfaction or distress you derive from your work.

Seven More Things You Can Do Now to Answer this One Question That Matters:

1. Take the time to consider your current level of job satisfaction. What role do you play (internal factors) and what role do others (external factors) play in this current state? How much of it is within the scope of your control and how much is not? What is one thing you can do / will do to make a shift in the right direction?

2. Initiate a conversation with a trusted friend at work about how easy you are to work with and what they perceive as your reputation among the team and across the organization. What value can you gain from this insight?

3. Identify your top three stakeholders at work and consider what it is that they expect of you. Do you meet these expectations consistently, sometimes, or rarely? What role does your answer play in your current level of job satisfaction?

4. Solicit input from your key stakeholders about their perception of how easy you are to work with. Encourage them to identify one thing you can do *more of* and one thing you can do *less of* to improve your capacity to collaborate.

5. Initiate a conversation with your peer group and or full team about what role personal accountability plays in job satisfaction and team success. Encourage them to add other accountability behaviors to the list of 10 presented in this article.

6. Invest the time to not only set doable goals, but also to track your progress. Small, consistent steps in the right direction over time go a long way in improving job satisfaction and impact.

7. Download the free Navigator Inventory 2.0, Building an Accountability Mindset assessment from the WorkChoice Solutions website (www.workchoicesolutions.com key words, Learning Resources, Leadership Assessments) and ask your entire team to complete it. Initiate a follow-up conversation around what the scores mean to group success and satisfaction and include a discussion around how the group can help boost the team's overall score.

CLOSING THOUGHT

CONGRUENCE MATTERS

Maria was a mid-level manager who like most 40-something professionals, was feeling overworked and a bit stressed. Her busy schedule juggling the many demands of career and family seemed to be accelerating. One day on her way to work she realized that she had forgotten about an important meeting that she was to attend for her boss. At about that point she also realized that the meeting was in fifteen minutes, and that she was at least twenty minutes away from the office.

Frustrated and more stressed, she approached the next intersection and found herself second in line at the traffic light, which had just turned red. Anxious, she began to tap on the steering wheel and repeatedly looked at her watch. As the light turned green, the car in front of her stalled. She grew even more frustrated and anx-ious. Just as the light turned yellow, the driver of the car in front of her restarted the car and darted through the yellow light, leaving Maria at the red light for a second time.

By now, Maria was quite agitated and ready to scream. She was surely going to be late for the meeting. Again she tapped the steer-ing wheel and anxiously looked at her watch. She was going to make it through the intersection this time she thought. Just as the light turned green, a school bus pulled into the intersection from the other direc-tion and proceeded to signal a pick-up or drop-off with its flashing red lights.

When no children appeared to be getting on or getting off of the bus, Maria became furious and began to blow the horn and shout at the bus driver. When this didn't seem to work, she rolled down her window and began to scream a few obscenities at the bus driver. Just as she thought that the bus was about to move, a loud pounding noise came from the back of her car. In a split second, a police officer appeared at her car window and proceeded to physi-cally remove her from the car, placing her in handcuffs, and putting her in the back of his police cruiser.

Maria became hysterical. Not only was she going to miss the meeting; she was sitting handcuffed in the back of a police car!

The policeman called his supervisor to the scene in an effort to get her to calm down. After a few minutes, the police supervisor took Maria from the cruiser and removed her handcuffs. He explained that the first police officer had been right behind her at the light and had observed her irrational behavior. "More impor-tantly" he said, the officer noticed the bumper stickers on her car proclaiming things like – *Serenity Now, Practice Random Acts of Kindness, and Patience is a Virtue* – and in light of her behavior was convinced that the car was stolen.

Great leaders don't put out mixed or contradictory messages about their values. They operate from a level of clarity and values-driven purpose that allow them to lead with congruence and to walk their talk every day. Every one of us possesses this level of power. Sure – it's easy to forget, get distracted, or even be afraid of our power. Nelson Mandela quoted Marianne Williamson in his1994 inaugural speech, saying "Our deepest fear is that we are powerful beyond measure. It is our light, not our darkness, that most frightens us." In being open to this truth, we not only discover why congruence matters, but we also help our teams and all of those around us to do the same.

What do your work and life related bumper stickers say about you? Can people tell your values by your actions? If someone were follow-ing you, would they think your car was stolen?

Team Discussion Questions

- Which of the articles resonated most with you?

- What were the most important lessons that you learned?

- What were the most important reminders that you uncovered?

- How do these lessons or reminders apply to us as leaders? As an organization? As a team?

- What are some options for applying the lessons?

- How will our approach to leadership be different?

- What should we do more of? What should we do less of?

- What should we stop doing? What should we start doing?

- What do we want to be known for as leaders?

- What's the cost of not taking action?

A Sampling of What Clients Say About David O'Brien's Expertise and Value

"David O'Brien designed and facilitated an enjoyable and insightful retreat for our senior leadership team that exceeded our expectations. It was an energizing and professionally stimulating experience that will have lasting value. It is a pleasure to work with David and we look forward to collaborating with him again in the future."

—CEO, Catholic Charities, Archdiocese of Hartford

"David O'Brien has a dynamic, interactive, collaborative style that immediately engages participants and puts them at ease. His breadth of knowledge of leadership topics and team dynamics along with his maneuverability in the moment make him one of the key facilitators in our High Potential Leadership Program."

—Vice President & Global Head of Learning and Development, AWAC Services Company a Member Company of Allied World

"David O'Brien delivered a power-house presentation during our recent "all-employee" offsite event. Our employees are still raving about it and have said that he is the best speaker we've ever had! He took the time to understand our company, our culture, our mission and incorporated all of that into his extremely motivating, educational, ENTERTAINING, and inspirational talk. He has a way of connecting with people in a way that is genuine, comfortable, and engaging.

—*Director of Operations, The Walker Group*

"Dave O'Brien of Work Choice Solutions provided us with leadership training customized to our needs. You could piece together a dozen "canned" training programs and still not come close to achieving the same result. Training was delivered with energy and sincerity which kept people engaged and motivated."

—*President, CemcoLift Co.*

"Of all the OD or Educational consultants that we have worked with at Saint Mary's you have done the most thorough research and completely understood our culture and our educational needs. This allowed you to design a program that was right on target and exceeded our expectations. Thank you for taking the time to get to know us and for designing a program which was highly customized".

—*VP, Human Resources, Saint Mary's Hospital*

"Thank you for the great work with us. You are terrific to work with and your insights, perspective, timeliness, flexibility and willingness to share made the leadership development program successful. Your personal dedication to the success of each session was very impressive. People felt that you were part of the team".

—*Divisional Vice President, Mass Mutual Financial Group*

"WorkChoice Solutions was our best choice for creating a meaningful and lasting cultural change within our group. Dave O'Brien's ability to understand our issues and to create substantive and relevant solutions has created a formula for sustained impact and success. Unlike many firms, WorkChoice Solutions is genuinely invested in positive outcomes well beyond the sale or delivery of services".

—*Vice President, Human Resources, U. S. Airways*

"Dave O'Brien's logical, practical and insightful approach to Leadership is very impactful. His passion and lighthearted approach helped to keep our team truly engaged throughout the training. I HIGHLY recommend Dave to assist any organization with their Leadership Development efforts. He is always willing to take a personal approach and not just deliver a canned presentation."

—Regional HR Director, Avery Dennison Corporation

"WorkChoice Solutions listened to our requirements and delivered results that were measurable and sustainable. The Performance Coaching program completely met the organization's needs for a higher level of productivity and the individual's concerns of performance improvement. Of particular note is the excellent work done by Dave O'Brien with the leader to increase his self-awareness and commitment to action plans involving new behaviors and change in general".

—HR Director, OTIS Elevator Co.

"We're glad we made a connection with WorkChoice Solutions. David O'Brien is a pleasure to work with. He does a remarkable job of soliciting feedback from his audience and tailoring his expertise to the unique needs of each individual. The leadership workshops he delivers to our members are always impressive. Attendees not only receive a rewarding experience, they walk away with information and practical tools that they can apply right away."

—Director of Membership & Training, Conecticut Association of Nonporifts

"Dave O'Brien hit the ball out of the park at our Tri-State Leadership Conference. His presentation moved the group to actively participate and learn. He was engaging, made some really good points and was very well prepared. Today people still make mention of his good work and how they have been able to apply his material."

—State Director President, Massachusetts Council of SHRM

"Dave O'Brien's Deliberate Leadership in a Distracted World breakfast keynote at our recent Business Expo was engaging and very well received. If you want to inspire a crowd with some great leadership tips and stories, look no further then Dave O'Brien. He talks about Leadership in a way that everyone can relate to and understand regardless of whether you're a CEO or a front line Supervisor. Dave leaves his audience upbeat and motivated to take action".

—*President, Greater New Haven Chamber of Commerce*

"In our HR profession, we speak of the emerging new workplace that "works for everyone". Dave O'Brien has been a pioneer thought leader for the past decade, preparing us for this revolution with his focus on human development, leadership and living/speaking your values at work. Dave brings his "whole self" to this work . . . Body, mind and spirit . . . . And his vision helps us articulate these dimensions of ourselves while we are at work. I always feel better about our chances as human beings in a broken institution (work) to rise above, respect one another and really create great organizations after being in Dave's presence. He is truly a gifted speaker who has been lead to this work, shoulders it, and makes us all the better in the process."

—*President, HRLA-SHRM Chapter*

"What Dave O'Brien brings to an organization goes way beyond the fact he is knowledgeable and talented at delivering an engaging program. Critical to the positive impact he creates is his ability to quickly earn trust and build rapport with all manner of people. His authenticity reflects his courage to "show up" as himself and, in my mind, does several things: It gives others permission to be their true selves (huge!); it disarms the Victims, Critics and Bystanders (necessary!); it shows respect for others through his automatic assumption that they will not take advantage of the vulnerability he entrusts them with (rare!) And it models strength (trusting yourself to handle rejection) and conviction. Dave is truly a special person and I consider myself very fortunate to have the opportunity to work with him and to call him my friend."

—*HR Director, CT Municipality*

The Navigator's Handbook:
101 Leadership Lessons for Work and Life

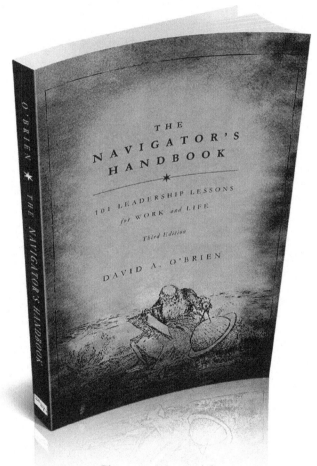

To get your copy visit
www.DavidOnAmazon.com

Made in the USA
Middletown, DE
22 May 2019